BL 6.2

PRECISION HIGH SCHOOL
A Dynamic Charter High School
3906 E. Broadway, #104
Phoenix, AZ 85040

Teenage Refugees From

RUSSIA

Speak Out

IN THEIR OWN VOICES

Teenage Refugees From

RUSSIA

Speak Out

TATYANA ZAMENOVA

THE ROSEN PUBLISHING GROUP, INC.
NEW YORK

Published in 1995 by The Rosen Publishing Group, Inc.
29 East 21st Street, New York, New York 10010

First Edition
Copyright © 1995 by The Rosen Publishing Group, Inc.

All rights reserved. No part of this book may be reproduced in any form without permission in writing from the publisher, except by a reviewer.

Manufactured in the United States of America.

Library of Congress Cataloging-in-Publication Data

Zamenova, Tatyana.
   Teenage refugees from Russia speak out / Tatyana Zamenova.
     p.   cm. — (In their own voices)
   Includes bibliographical references and index.
   ISBN 0-8239-1846-7
   1. Russian American teenagers—Juvenile literature. 2. Refugees—United
States—Juvenile literature.   I. Title. II. Series.
E184.R9B34 1994
973'.049171—dc20
                                              94-23654
                                                 CIP
                                                     AC

Contents

The Russian flag flies over the Kremlin, the former Soviet government headquarters. The Russian flag took the place of the Soviet flag, which was removed after Soviet President Mikhail Gorbachev resigned in 1991.

INTRODUCTION

The complexity of Russia, its enormous size, turbulent history, and incredible cultural legacy have always drawn attention to it. It is a country of tremendous scale and remoteness—stretching from the Arctic Ocean to the borders of China, Mongolia, and the Middle Eastern nations. It covers more than a seventh of the earth's surface, making it the world's largest single nation-state.

While European countries were undergoing great changes during the Middle Ages and the Renaissance, Russia was invaded and ruled by Tatars and Mongolians for almost 300 years. Perhaps the most crippling effect of Mongol rule was that Russia became increasingly isolated from Western Europe. The Mongol practice of collecting tribute payments in silver from Russian cities was successfully challenged by Ivan III, tsar of Russia from 1462 to 1505. In 1556, the rule of the Tatars was brought to an end by Ivan IV, also known as Ivan the Terrible. Defeat of the Tatars brought the entire Volga River within the borders of Russia.

Russia became a great European power at the beginning of the 18th century. This period was dominated by the processes of expansion, Westernization, and economic modernization. The Russian tsar Peter the Great won a twenty-year battle with invading Swedish forces and established his frontiers on the shores of the Baltic and the Gulf of Finland in 1721. The gaining of a foothold on the Baltic Sea gave Russia direct access to Western Europe. Expansion southward and westward brought many different national groups such as Jews, Poles, Ukrainians, Crimean Tatars, and Lithuanians into the Russian fold, creating a multiethnic empire.

Peter the Great brought Western concepts of administration, industry, and warfare to Russia. He required his nobles to change their Oriental robes for Western clothes, cut their long beards, and become more like Europeans. He brought the best architects from Europe to build his dream city on a swamp—St. Petersburg, which became one of Europe's most beautiful cities. Now its population is approximately five million people. The capital of the country is the ancient city of Moscow, which dates back to 1147. Now it is one of the largest cities in the world, with a population of approximately ten million people.

Vladimir Ilich Lenin led the October Revolution of 1917, which overthrew the monarchy of Nicholas II. The tsarist regime was destroyed in Russia, and Lenin proclaimed the first socialist state in the

Семь раз отмерь,

один раз отрежь.

ENGLISH TRANSLATION FROM RUSSIAN:
Measure seven times, cut once.

world. In 1918, his Russian Social Democratic Labor Party, or Bolsheviks, changed its name to the Russian Communist Party.

According to Communist ideals, everything in the state belongs to everyone. People were allowed to have only limited personal possessions. Rules and restrictions controlled how much people could own. The Communist Party dominated every aspect of the lives of Russian citizens. One quotation describing communism says, "All people of the country are equal in their rights, but there are some people who are more equal." "Some people" would seem to refer to members of the Communist Party.

Young Russian girls sport the uniform of the Young Pioneers, the youth division of the Communist Party in the former Soviet Union.

While all citizens age 18 or older had the right to vote, voters usually had the choice of only one candidate who had been handpicked by Communist Party officials. The Party also selected factory directors, newspaper editors, directors of institutes, and other holders of powerful positions. In 1922, Russia became a republic in the Union of Soviet Socialist Republics, or U.S.S.R. The U.S.S.R. consisted of fifteen separate republics, fourteen of which were annexed to Russia.

Lenin was succeeded in 1924 by Joseph Stalin.

During his reign, lasting almost thirty years, Stalin made the U.S.S.R. into an economic and political world power. However, his regime was also infamous for its ruthlessness. Oppression came to a climax in the 1930s and 1940s when he sentenced fifteen million people to exile and forced them to work in Siberia's mines and forests. In most cases his victims were exiled without reason. This period was marked by these sweeping arrests, known as the Stalinist purges, in which millions of people lost their lives.

The years after Stalin's death were characterized by the continuing spread of Soviet influence in many parts of the world. The Cold War, the ongoing struggle for power between the United States and the Soviet Union, became the major force in world politics. Domestically, Soviet leaders had learned important lessons from Stalin's excesses, but repression of civil rights and liberties continued. The K.G.B., or Soviet security police, was the agency most often responsible for controlling the population. New prohibitions, new rules and regulations, and new red tape made life very difficult. Emigration was usually prohibited.

Many people, both inside and outside Russia, had come to see the Soviet system as increasingly dysfunctional. Mikhail Gorbachev, who became leader of the U.S.S.R. in 1985, shared this view. He initiated a far-reaching program of political and economic reforms that he called *perestroika*, or restructuring. Gorbachev proposed multicandidate elections, less censorship, and an end to the political domination of the Communist Party. Economically, he proposed allowing a limited amount of private enterprise and making price structures more flexible.

Gorbachev's reforms had far-ranging effects. The Soviet grip on Eastern Europe slipped, and Communist regimes collapsed in countries such as Poland and East Germany. At home, the Soviet economy could not handle the many changes. Food shortages and strikes became frequent. Inflation soared. The other Soviet republics began to seek more freedom from the central powers. Many republics wanted to break away from the Union.

Frightened by their loss of power, high-ranking members of the armed services, security forces, and other agencies of the Communist Party tried to seize power from Gorbachev in 1991. Boris Yeltsin, president of the Russian government, opposed the coup. It collapsed soon after it started. The U.S.S.R. was destroyed a short time afterward, with Russia and the other republics becoming independent nations.

Yeltsin, now the president of the Russian Federation, has initiated many of his own reforms. In fact, he is even more committed than Gorbachev to moving the country toward a market economy. He also passed a new constitution, based on the French constitution. For his actions, he faced strong opposition from certain members of

McDonald's and other fast-food chains such as Pizza Hut can now be found on the streets of Moscow. Twenty years ago, it would have been unimaginable to find such symbols of American capitalism in Russia.

Russian teenagers in Moscow drink glasses of Pepsi from a machine. The policies of former Soviet President Mikhail Gorbachev led to greater openness to Western influences.

parliament. Fighting between the opposition and forces loyal to Yeltsin broke out on the streets of Moscow in October 1993. Yeltsin maintained power when he defeated his opponents with his assault on the Russian White House.

The disintegration of the Communist system and the shift to a new economic and political system has not been easy for the Russian people. Extreme food shortages, high prices, and political instability continue to be features of their lives.

*   *   *

Some of the teenagers interviewed for this book asked that their photographs not be used. Others wanted the world to know who they are. In all cases, we have used only the students' first names in order to protect their privacy.♦

Maria came to the United States when she was thirteen. Her parents were not anti-Communist, but they were free-thinkers and had many friends from other countries.

Her life in the United States has not been easy. She dropped out of high school, but is now planning to go back to school. She writes music, plays the guitar, and sings. She enjoys life and is looking forward to exploring it. She is talented, beautiful, and assertive.

1

MARIA
MY MOM AND THE KGB

My name is Maria. I grew up in Leningrad, which is now St. Petersburg. The family was my mother, my grandmother, and me at first, and then my stepfather and his two sons. I went to a French school in Leningrad. The atmosphere in school was very different from the U.S. Here you grow up to be free, you always have choices. In Russia everything is very strict. The teachers have power over the kids. They could beat us up if they wanted to.

It was a very political time. We had a class called Political Information, starting in the first grade. It was an anti-American class, and we had to attend this class every week for 20 minutes. We had to look through newspapers and cut out articles about how bad it is to live in America.

We also had a class called Civil Defense, start-ing in second grade. We were taught what to do in

Russian students study English in a Moscow classroom. According to many Russian teenagers who attend school in the U.S., Russian schools are stricter than American schools.

case the bad, scary Americans decided to drop a bomb on us. We had to learn how to defend ourselves; we had to shoot rifles and learn how to use gas masks, and a lot of kids started having nightmares. We made fun of it somewhat, but it was supposed to be very important. Once in a while a siren would go off in school to indicate that war had started, and we would have to put on our gas masks and go down to the basement.

Every chance our teachers got, they would try to feed us some political propaganda. In fact, I remember the very first class that I went to—it was the first grade, my first hour of school—our teacher showed us a picture of Ronald Reagan. He was goofing off, because he was an actor, you know, and both of his fingers were stuck in his ears. It was a really silly picture, but the teacher set it up on the board and said, "Kids, do you know who this is?" Of course we didn't know, and she said, "Well, this is the President of the United States, Ronald Reagan, and do you know what he's doing?" And we said, "No," and she said, "Well, every time he hears the word 'peace,' he tries to plug up his ears." So that was the very first impression of the United States that I got from school. The very first three words we had to learn were mother, motherland, and Lenin, but not necessarily in that order; actually it was more like Lenin, motherland, and mother.

My mother was always very free about speaking her mind. She always tried to separate right and wrong for me, and she had a lot of friends who were considered public enemies, who were in jail or exile for political reasons. She always had a lot of foreign friends. One of the reasons we left Russia was because the K.G.B. was after my mother twenty-four hours a day. Our phone was tapped, and they followed her around. Ironically, when we moved in with my stepfather we were living right across from the K.G.B. headquarters in Leningrad. They called her in a bunch of times, and they tried to scare her into saying something that was not true. They tried to get her to name her friends and to admit doing things that she had never done. People at work avoided her; nobody wanted to be her friend. She wasn't in any political movement that revolted against the government; she just had a lot of different kinds of friends and she read whatever she wanted to read.

In school I was afraid of saying something wrong, because I didn't want to get my mother in trouble. I was always thinking, "Maybe I shouldn't be saying this in this sort of company, because who knows where they'll go next and who they'll tell." I was always hanging out with Mom and her friends and I have a perfect memory, so I remembered all of their political jokes. My parents told me to keep my mouth shut in front of the wrong people.

In school we had a teacher who was a total fanatic. She was a Stalinist, and she tried to feed it to us every chance she got. One time she said, "Kids, do you know what day it is today?" And we

Vladimir Ilich Lenin speaks to the new Soviet Army in Moscow in 1919. Lenin proclaimed Russia the first socialist state in the world.

said, "No, we don't." And she said, "Well, today is a day attributed to Georgian heroes. Can you name any?" We couldn't think of any. And she said, "You are forgetting Joseph Stalin." And we said, "What kind of hero was he?" And she said, "You've been misinformed. Everybody makes mistakes, and the reason Stalin did a couple of things wrong was because he was misinformed. He had a person working for him who was an English spy, and he was trying to misinform Stalin." By then we were in fourth grade, so we didn't believe any of it. We told our parents what this teacher had said. And that was the very first time in that very strict school that we actually got a teacher fired.

Our class was the first rebellious class in the history of that school. We got really fed up, and we started doing everything against the rules. The whole class started skipping the Civil Defense and Political Information classes. We simply didn't show up. A bunch of teachers quit, pretty much because they couldn't deal with us anymore. We did really nasty things to them.

Besides the political information and all that gibberish, we also had literature, French literature and grammar, chemistry, and physics at sixth grade, and after sixth grade we had mathematics, writing, and recreational things like drawing, music, singing. History of the Soviet Union was pretty stupid because they omitted everything that Russia has done wrong, which is pretty much everything. Once we got on the subject of communism. One smart aleck asked the teacher exactly what communism was, and she had a hard time explaining it: There will be no money, everybody will have everything for free, nobody will have to go to work, everything will be done by machines. The whole class got up and started screaming, "We don't want communism!" It was such a shock that our teacher didn't know what to do. Later we got a five-hour lecture about it from the principal.

In Leningrad, until I was about four, we shared an apartment with a guy and his wife. The guy used to be a warden at a concentration camp, so you can imagine the kind of person he was. Then we moved in with my stepfather, which was a total joke because it was 125 square feet and there were five of us. Then we moved into another apartment where we had two rooms for ourselves, and my stepfather made them into four rooms. We had to share the apartment with two other families. One family were criminals, and apparently the entire police department of Leningrad was looking for them. We found a dead body in our basement. There were constant fights; they would beat each other up with empty bottles. They would lock us in our rooms. Only when the cops finally threatened them did they move.

One of my mother's best friends waited for seven years before she got permission to come to the U.S. That gave my parents something to think about. They saw that things couldn't remain the way they were going. They saw a change coming; they were afraid there would be bloodshed and a lot of problems. Mom was having bad problems with the K.G.B., and she didn't want me to have to face the same kind of persecution.

We had to fake a lot of documents. We had to fake an invitation from Israel. Just when we were ready to give up, we finally got the permit. September 8, 1988, was the day we left Moscow. At the airport they checked every single bag you had. They strip-searched you. We finally got on the plane, and we had no idea where we were going. Our first stop was Austria. We stayed in Vienna for about twenty days, and we went to every single museum, opera, and play. Since we were sup-

In Totsk, Russia, visitors gather at a monument to the Cold War. The monument marks the site where a test nuclear bomb was exploded in 1951.

posed to be Jewish, we had to learn about all the Jewish holidays. We had to say that we were of Jewish descent. The thing that saved us is that we had other reasons to leave Russia besides being Jewish, like Mom's problems with the K.G.B.

We had friends in Worcester, Massachusetts, who sponsored us. I started school fifteen days after I arrived in the U.S. One of the biggest problems I had was not knowing how to dress. In Russia, you pretty much wear what they give you. I didn't have any good clothes at all. All my clothes were totally out of style. People made fun of me but I had no idea why. In Russia, you wear the same thing as long as it's clean. In America, you can't wear the same thing again for about two weeks.

My family was having a lot of problems, and Mom and I got our own apartment in Worcester. Then she decided to go to Rutgers University in New Jersey. She is studying there now. I entered a different high school in Highland Park, New Jersey. My first year of high school was cool, but the second year I started having a lot of problems with my mom. I started doing whatever I wanted and getting into a lot of trouble.

Finally, I got together with my mom. She said, "Why don't you go to Alaska?" That's how I ended up in Alaska for two months. It was great. I got to do so many things I never dreamt I would do. It was beautiful. I got to fly helicopters, fly planes, go fishing, go hunting, go boating. I worked as a volunteer with the National Park Service and as a Russian interpreter.

Now I'm moving into my own apartment in New Brunswick, New Jersey. I'm going back to school for my G.E.D., I'm going to college, and I'm going to get a job. When I can't find a bright side, I look at the funny side of things. I figure that so many bad things have happened to me in my life, I might as well stick around and see what happens next. What keeps me alive is the challenge of finding happiness.◆

Marianna is a well-spoken, thoughtful young woman who lives in Brooklyn, New York. She has thought a great deal about what it means to be a refugee and to be Russian. She talks of some of the difficulties she and her family have had in adjusting to life in the United States.

MARIANNA
TOURING ST. PETERSBURG

I am from St. Petersburg. It's known as the second capital of Russia. It is a very nice city. I am 17.

We lived far from the center of the city in a residential district. My parents, my brother, and I had a two-bedroom apartment.

In Russia, the system of education is very different. Here you go to elementary school, junior high, and then high school. In Russia there is only one school; first you go to elementary, then to middle, then to high school, the same building, same school, same teachers. Everybody knows you from the time you are seven years old until you are sixteen. We studied the same things there that we do here, but the system is completely different. Here you may choose to study art if you like, music if you like, or even mathematics. But in Russia you have no choice. You have to study mathematics, music, art, history, geography, Russian, and a foreign language. It is probably better than in the U.S. because they go deeper into the subject. Kids here study chemistry for one year. Kids in Russia study it for four years. When Russian kids come to the U.S. it is no problem for them to do well. Sometimes it seems as if Russians are more intelligent, but it's just a matter of the education system.

I miss our school very much. We had very nice teachers. Sometimes at larger schools propaganda is a problem, but we didn't feel it at all. Our teachers taught history from the historical point of view, not from the point of view of Soviet leaders. I never felt the threat.

I started school in 1983, and the changes began in 1985. Everything was changing, and that is probably why we didn't experience any problems. My brother is three years older than I. He studied several subjects, the history of the Communist Party, for example, that I never had to study. We had new subjects like the history of European civilization, or the beginnings of Christianity, or the fundamental principles of the world.

I can only credit my English to my Russian school. It was a specialized school, and we could study different languages than most kids. Without that, I think I would have died. The American accent is special; it's different from what I learned. You don't understand TV or anything. You are like a

In St. Petersburg, a street musician plays for onlookers against the backdrop of the city's magnificent architecture.

newborn child who doesn't know anything about this world, but at the same time you are sixteen years old and supposed to know things. You can't express yourself. You can't ask for what you want. It is depressing, and I just thank my school and my old English teacher. She made me study very hard.

We had many interesting activities. For example, we visited the theater museum. At first we just listened to lectures about the theaters and performances of fifty years ago. Then we tried to stage something ourselves. We learned about the city of St. Petersburg. It is an incredibly beautiful city. It was founded in 1703 during the Russian-Swedish **29**

War. And during the following two hundred years it became not only the capital but one of the most beautiful capitals in the world. There are so many things to see. It is very beautiful, and at the same time mystical. I miss it greatly. It is a city everyone should see.

I used to a be a guide/interpreter there. I went to a special school to be a guide.

We had lectures about the history of Russia and how Peter the Great built the city as a fortress against the Swedish. Then he decided to make it the capital because he thought Moscow was too Russian. Until the 18th century, Russia was self-contained, and Peter wanted to open it up to the world. He brought many masters from Germany and sculptors and architects from all over the world to build the city. He wanted it to be a European city. He even called it the northern Venice. He wanted to build canals like those in Venice, but the soil prevented him.

After we had our lectures, we toured the city and the museums. We walked all over the city and tried to remember who built this building and when. Then we got a kind of diploma that allowed us to show the city to groups of teenagers. In my school there were kids from all over the world, from Australia, from Great Britain, and from the United States. Mostly English-speaking countries. My school was strong in English, so there were many students from other countries there. We showed them the city as best as we could.

I played tennis at a club once a week; a trainer taught us how to play. Also I went skiing. In the winter our family usually went to a very nice place not far from Finland, near the Gulf. We rented a little house for the week, like when people in the States go to upstate New York to ski and rest.

My family is very close. That's the way it's always been. If my brother or I have problems, we always go to our family because these people understand us and know how to help. Most Russian teens in the United States come from Jewish families. They are more closely united with each other than others. The family ties are strong. I love my family, and I miss them when I don't see them. I can't live without them. When I think about going to college, I try to imagine myself without them. I have been with them all my life.

The decision to leave Russia was pretty spontaneous. The family didn't decide, "Okay guys, let's go to the United States because life here is terrible." In Russia, people began emigrating to the United States in the early seventies. The question of emigration always existed. In my family we were thinking about it even in the seventies before my brother was born. My mother told me that back then the decision was made to stay. The situation was completely different for us in the seventies. My father was twenty-six years old with a Ph.D., and my mother worked. They had whatever they needed: an apartment, a car, a little vacation house. They felt themselves to be upper middle

In 1994, Russian university students protest inadequate funding and a government policy that requires them to interrupt their studies to serve in the military.

class. Then things changed dramatically. My father is a radio engineer. He was one of the designers of the landing system on a spaceship. My mother was an engineer in heating systems and operations. The point is that they were working for the government. In the eighties, when the government changed, they lost funding for their projects. They were out of work. It changed our lives pretty dramatically. For example, we couldn't go where we used to because of money.

When the political situation in our country changed, our family discussed it. Teachers discussed it in school. Parents discussed it at their jobs or with their colleagues. Sometimes I asked my father, "Why didn't they change these things before now? Why didn't they tell the government that what they were doing was not right?" And he would say, "Don't forget that only a short time ago, in the fifties, during the Cold War, if you said something like that, you said goodbye to your family. You would disappear."

In the eighties, the economy was not what it should have been. It was as if something had broken. It was like a storm. People began to talk. The country is now very unstable; nobody knows what the president will do; no one knows who will win the elections. This is the result of democracy. There is no stability. Who knows how long it will last? Forty or fifty years, maybe.

That is one of the reasons why my parents decided to come to the U.S. Like all parents, they care about their children, and they wanted me and my brother to get a good education and to be a little bit freer than they were.

When I call my friends in Russia and ask how they are, they tell me they are in college now and I am only in high school. I feel I am not at the same level. They say, sure, there are problems in Russia, but our parents feel those problems, not us. My friends are pretty wealthy, so they do not feel the economic issues that most people feel. But the country is divided into two parts. One part—a small part, actually—is wealthy, they have money, they have millions of dollars, no troubles. At the same time, the majority of people who worked in the factories or were teachers have nothing. Their incomes are extremely low. They eat anything they can get. Everything is very expensive.

Probably my parents were right in coming to the U.S. It is very hard in Russia. But those who stay continue to work. Over here my parents are trying to find jobs, but the problem is that they are in their late forties. My father has many friends in several universities, but there don't seem to be any possibilities. He's trying to find something that is related to his field. He taught in college for five years after he received his Ph.D., and then he switched from the theoretical to the practical. He's looking in both areas, but there is nothing. And there is no way my mom could find work as an engineer here. She's forty-seven, and women don't generally work in her field in the United States. She is studying to be a social worker. She is very communicative, and she cares about people. She is the kind of person who should be a social worker.

Many women were engineers in Russia: my mother, my aunt, my friend's mother. It was very common. In Russia, the whole system of education is different. Here the humanitarian subjects are studied more. In Russia the majority of time is spent on mathematics, chemistry, and physics. I remember in my last year in high school we had eight hours of mathematics every week, eight hours of physics, and about four hours of chemistry; but I only had four hours of literature and two hours of history. It was very different.◆

Tolia, seventeen, is one of many Russian Jews who have immigrated to the United States because of religious persecution in the former Soviet Union. Tolia grew up in Siberia, an area famous for its harsh climate and geographic isolation.

TOLIA
LIFE IN SIBERIA

My name is Tolia and I am 17 years old. I come from a place called Birsk. It is in Novosibirsk or New Siberia, approximately 2,500 miles from Moscow. My parents are originally from the same village in Moldova; it is called Asaki. They came to Birsk because my father studied to be a physicist at the state university there, and then he found a job in the Siberian branch of the Russian Academy of Sciences. I have one older brother. He and his wife live in the United States now also.

I attended public school in Russia. There were only state schools there. Now there are some private schools. I like to study. I especially like science and mathematics. I graduated from my school in Russia with a gold medal.

In Russia you attend school for eight or ten years. After you finish eight years you may enter a technical college, or you may continue your education and spend two more years in school, as I did. Then you may enter university. For me, entering the university was easy; having won the gold medal, I could enter by passing only one exam. I decided to go to the Novosibirsk State University because to go far from home was dangerous. Some universities in Moscow are not so good for Jews. For many years Jews could not enter these universities. There was discrimination. And in Moscow, things are hard economically.

We decided to emigrate because of the political situation in Russia. It is not stable; anything can happen. After we sent in our papers, it took about three and a half years to get permission to emigrate. We had relatives who invited us to the U.S.

I miss my friends in Russia very much. Except for my brother, I have nobody like them to talk to here. I just don't know what to talk about with Americans. The cultures are so different. I have been in the states for almost four months. I have a job here, and I am applying to universities.

I have some American friends because in Russia I went to a Jewish camp that was run by Americans. They were interested in understanding Russia. Russia is strange even for Russians. You can't understand it with your mind. It is an emotional experience.

Most Siberian students learn to cross-country ski. There is a proverb: If you live in Siberia, stay on the skis. Physical education in school included skiing in winter.

Mikhail Gorbachev was a very wise man, but he didn't do what he might have done. There were many clever, wise people near him, but he didn't believe them. Russia has a tradition of powerful people doing whatever they like. If you're the tsar or the head of government you don't have to listen to anybody else. About four years ago, Andrei Sakharov tried to tell us that we had to change the Russian constitution, and nobody would listen to him. If you read the constitution now, it's nonsense. I think it was written in 1977 or something, when Brezhnev was in power. It's very conservative.

My goals in the U.S. are to continue my education and improve my English. You see life differently when you're educated. I want to be an intelligent person; I want to be educated. But I don't want to forget the Russian language and culture. This is so important for me that I don't think I can live without it. We brought Russian books with us. We have a big Russian library.◆

Anastasia moved to the United States from St. Petersburg in 1989. She is a very talented young woman with diverse interests in the humanities. Her short stories and poems are frequently published in her high school's literary magazine. In 1992 she received a National Merit Award from Congress for her painting.

ANASTASIA
FAITH IN MYSELF

My name is Anastasia. I am 17 years old. Currently I live in Brooklyn, New York. I spent the first twelve years of my life in the center of Leningrad, now St. Petersburg. As a little child I remember always being happy. An only child, I grew up in a very warm, caring family with a liberal and intellectual atmosphere. I was an avid reader, and I loved drawing and writing poems. Besides my own creative world, my parents were always taking me to the Hermitage Museum, the Russian Museum, or to the Bolshoi Theater, where I fell in love with the ballet. In retrospect, I realize that I had a very special childhood. Because my parents were liberal, and because my mother had time to spend with me, I grew up in a home where I was safe and happy, where I could express myself according to who I am. Thus, I was absolutely free for the first seven years of my life.

I went to a special French school in Russia. I loved Russian literature, French, and art. I had wonderful teachers for all these subjects. Most schools in Russia are very strict. You can't freely express your own views. There was a great deal of favoritism. Students who were less creative or talented often were the teacher's favorites.

In religion, I was brought up liberally. I am Russian Orthodox, in other words, of Christian faith. But because any kind of religious activity was suppressed in Russia, I did not become traditionally religious.

Our actual living conditions in Russia were rather poor. I grew up on Tchaikovsky Street, named after the Russian composer. Four of us— my parents, my grandmother, and I—lived in a small apartment, one room and a tiny kitchen. It was difficult living with so little room, but we managed somehow. It was really cozy in a way. For as long as I can remember, we always had a problem getting food. Although the food was of very good quality, coming from all the rich repub- lics in the former U.S.S.R., such as Ukraine, it was so hard to get. Fruits were scarce in Leningrad in the summer, and in the winter there were none at all. Vegetables and meat had to be hunted down in the stores, and then people waited in long lines to get them. My family could afford to eat fairly well because my grandmother was a dentist and my father a designer for a book publishing com- pany. We could afford to travel throughout the

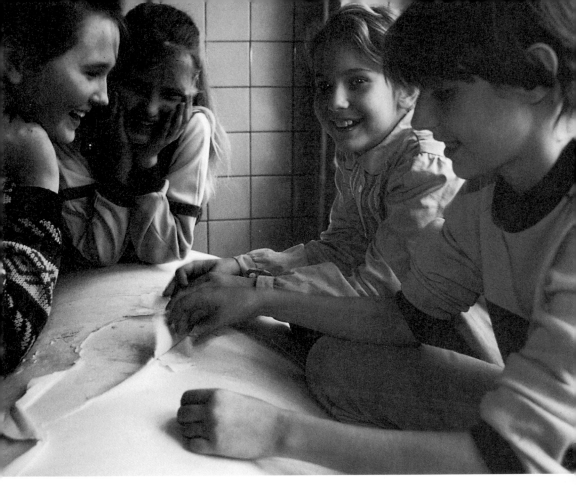

Students at the Lisse School in Moscow work on a project.

country, to the Black Sea and the Baltic Sea, but that was it. That was all a normal family could afford, and most families were much poorer. But I love Russia with all my heart, because I will always remember the way it was in my childhood.

When I was twelve I suddenly found out we were moving to the United States. This was the most exciting thing that had ever happened to me. We spent two months in Vienna, then two months in Italy. I saw the real Europe and was fascinated and overwhelmed. Life in Europe seemed heaven after Russia. People seemed healthy, happy. Supermarkets were filled with food. I can't remember how many museums and churches I saw. But with all this luxury, my parents and I were always on edge, always worried about our visa. If we were not accepted in the U.S., we would have had no country at all.

But we got through this period. After waiting for four months we finally made it to the United States. In all honesty, the U.S. did not make a very good first impression on me. Brooklyn, which is the part of the U.S. I saw first, seemed dull. On the other hand, I fell in love with Manhattan immediately. Living here for five years, I have learned to love the United States dearly. To me it represents freedom, health, and fun. Of course, you have to work hard to earn the freedom and fun you get. If you want to be at the very top, as I do, it takes all your energy, but that's what I really like about this country: It gives you so much in return.

I've been going to St. Anne's School for four years, and I feel very lucky to be at one of the best schools in the States. My career plan formed in my head long ago. I want to be an animator and a writer, and now I feel certain that I can achieve my goals. I think I'd like to live in New York City all my life, although I'd like to travel and see the world.

I love being a Russian-American, though I feel more Russian at heart. I can keep my Russian culture and at the same time try to absorb the best of of the U.S.

I speak Russian all the time at home. In my family we rarely eat traditional Russian food—except potato dumplings and borscht, a delicious vegetable soup with beets. So this is my life now, and I am happy to have gotten this far in life. The United States has given me faith in myself. I still keep in touch with some of my Russian friends, and I write to them about my new life and how much it has changed me. I think the U.S. is the best place for me to live right now, because here I can pretty well see my future, and I know it's only up to me what I'll make of my life.

Americans made a good impression on me from the start. Now, as I get to know them better, I think they're wonderful people, friendly, open-minded. Although the U.S. has a very young culture, I respect its ability to adapt and absorb other cultures, from East or West. I know Russia is not the same as when I left, so I think there is no point in returning to that desolate country. But I still have the Russian spirit.

I think the hardest part of being a refugee is to find a job. This was particularly hard for my parents. When we first arrived we lived with our Russian friends in Brooklyn. Then after a couple of months we found ourselves a nice apartment in a beautiful Hasidic neighborhood. But my parents were still unemployed. Finally my father started studying to be a dental technician, and my mother found a job in a home care company. She worked there for about two years. Mom then decided to become a lawyer's assistant. She took English and law courses at New York Technical College. The English-speaking environment made her English stronger and gave her self-assurance. My father unfortunately was deprived of this opportunity because his job didn't give him any time to study English seriously.◆

Russian students say their good-byes in front of a Moscow apartment complex after school. In many parts of Russia, good housing is difficult to obtain.

Julia, nineteen, has lived in the United States for seven years. She struggled in the past with the clash between her Russian and American experiences, but has now come to terms with her dual identity.

The events of October, 1993, when Russia was gripped by a struggle for power, were difficult for Julia and her family. She watched the events on American television, knowing that her father and half-sister were in Moscow.

JULIA
A MOUSE AMONG CATS

On August 26, 1987, I thought I had become an American. Wearing a pale red dress with long, white old-fashioned socks, hair cut short, I stepped out of a small plane in Providence, Rhode Island. Unsure of my future, unaware of possible complications, curious, hopeful and scared, I looked upon American land. At age twelve, I stood before a smiling and crying crowd of friends and strangers.

Ever since I can remember, my family's goal was to emigrate from the Soviet Union because of the religious persecution of Jews. It was forbidden to practice religion or to study Hebrew, yet at the same time Jews were not allowed to leave the country. Although I attended a typical Russian school and wore the black school uniform (it was required), I never felt a part of the "system."

Russian soldiers help out with the potato harvest in the Russian village of Ramenskoye, near Moscow. The potato is a mainstay of the Russian diet.

This is how I remember my first day in kindergarten: Hundreds of cheerful, innocent kids running through school doors. Teachers were holding flowers and smiling at us. I thought nothing could go wrong until . . .

My classroom teacher asked each girl: "What is your nationality?" Each student in my class answered, "Russian," but I announced with pride, "I am Jewish." I was a Jew among Russians, and that was worse than being a mouse among cats.

Throughout my school years, I had to lead a double life—one in school, listening to the

Communist propaganda, and a very different life at home.

I always had to watch what I said, and to whom I talked. And I couldn't say at school, or even to my friends, what we had been discussing at home. As soon as my mother applied to leave the country, she lost her job with the Moscow Conservatory, where she had worked as professor of music for many years. She wasn't allowed to work for six years. The unfairness of my mother's being arrested for taking part in strikes exploded in my mind.

Although I supported my family struggle, many times I wished for a normal life. At times, I must admit I even wished to be Russian because of the overwhelming problems I had to deal with as a Jew. My life was a jail, and the only way to get out was to leave.

After being "Refuseniks" for six years, wading through unfulfilled promises from the Soviet bureaucracy, and withstanding continued emotional struggles for freedom, my family was finally given permission to leave the Soviet Union.

The moment Aeroflot 108 came to a stop on American soil, I stepped out, young, energetic, full of hope, and eager to learn. I had promised myself that I would not allow myself to be different again in my new society. I was determined to master the only language in the world that capitalizes the word 'I.' I thought that in order to become an American, I would have to forget my identity as a Russian. I can now laugh about the times when I followed everyone blindly, without questioning, when I thought that different meant low or rotten.

After living in the United States for six years, I have had a taste of two very distinct cultures. In the beginning, it was so important for me to feel part of the community that I was willing to compromise myself and my heritage. Now I am proud of who I am and where I come from.

I still think, dance, work, and have fun like a Russian. I tremble when I sing the old Russian songs. I have noticed that Americans value privacy and independence and don't emphasize camaraderie. It is very rare when one has sacred friends. I have been raised to think of friendship as a religion. In Russia, friends were a necessity of life. The relations within my family are tied with a metal knot. None of my American friends share the closeness that my mother and I share. There is no superficiality, no barrier standing between my family and me.

I'll never stop thinking and worrying about Russia. I feel an especially strong connection when Russia is in trouble. It's difficult even to describe what I experienced a year ago.

Imagine troops, soldiers in uniforms, tanks, gunshots and fires . . . on your street! Impossible! Yet that is exactly what I had to witness in October 1993, when CNN announced that Russia was in a state of crisis. I recognized the Moscow boulevards and alleys on TV as the places where I had learned

In October 1993, Russian soldiers fought a coup attempt by Communist hardliners who took over the Parliament building.

to walk, collected flowers, played with friends, and where I serenely and sadly walked with my father and baby sister for the last time. They were the avenues to which I said my good-bye seven years ago, not knowing if I'd ever see them again. But instead of sunshine, green grass, illuminated sidewalks, fountains, and happy kids playing, I saw soldiers with guns. My favorite ice cream shop was burning, and people were shouting and moaning as they were pushed off the sidewalks by tanks. I couldn't believe that Moscow's streets had been turned into open-air shooting ranges by their own citizens.

Two teenage boys practice their skateboarding skills on a Moscow street.

But knowing that my father and my half-sister still lived in Moscow brought the harsh reality home. I tried to keep scary thoughts out of my mind, but my anxiety was not relieved until I heard my dad's voice on the phone. Although he assured me that they were still in one piece, my fears didn't end. I wanted to walk through the front door of my father's house, throw my arms around my little sister, and see with my own eyes that they were unharmed.

I think if one good thing came out of this last Russian crisis, it is that the Russian people now know just how much harder they will need to fight in order to break the old order and establish a new one. And of course such things can't be changed at once. Many people ask me what I think about changes in Russia. We had left Moscow just before the process of *perestroika* began. But I personally think that not many things could really have changed. The mentality of people can't change just because some leader says it has to change.♦

Ilia, nineteen, moved to the United States in 1989 from St. Petersburg and now lives in Brookline, Massachusetts. Last year he entered the Massachusetts Institute of Technology. He is devoted to studying and working with computers. He spends most evenings at a laboratory at Harvard University. He is a well-read, thoughtful young man who loves poetry and music. He plays the guitar and sings beautiful songs. The things he values most in life are friendship, work, art, and family. He is a modest, sincere person.

ILIA
A LOST TRAVELER

Whenever a new acquaintance notices my accent, he asks, predictably, "Where are you from?" followed by the inevitable, "How do you like it here?" For over five years, I have been repeating the same reply with the precision of a tape recorder. "I moved here from Leningrad, Russia, x years ago, some things here I like, some I don't..." Except for the length of my stay, nothing changes in the response. Yet as time went by, a slow but sure internal change was going on, a change of views, attitudes, and perceptions, a change I could notice only in retrospect.

I came to this country five years ago. Unlike other immigrants, I never was really eager to leave my city. My life was pretty interesting. I attended good schools—one specialized in English and humanities and later math school. I had an opportunity to communicate with interesting people. But most important for me were my friends—people who were so close to me that I could hardly imagine anybody else taking their place.

But the political situation was getting worse. My father was frightened that it could become as bad as in Bosnia. The increasing number of anti-Semitic meetings with such slogans as "Kill the Jews— save Russia!" didn't add any hope for the situation to get better. So we decided to go.

After the initial hassles of settling passed, I found myself in a deep depression. Everything in this new place appeared in a negative light. The bread felt and tasted like cotton. Advertising per-meated streets, newspapers, and TV programs. The perpetual wailing of ambulance sirens echoed through my soul, leaving sharp, chilling streaks of fear.

To get me out of my depression, my father sent me to a summer camp. From the first day I was an outcast. Locked out of most activities by the language barrier, unfamiliar with basic games and customs, I quickly acquired the reputation of a dummy who doesn't even know how to play base-ball.

"Friend" is a word I do not often use. It means too much to me. I think, for example, one can't have many friends. The word stands for such a close, sincere, serious, permanent relationship that one usually has only one or two such people in one's life. And as I had expected, my new aquaintances couldn't replace my loss.

I came back from camp more depressed than when I left. In the two weeks remaining before the beginning of school, I rarely left the apartment. I spent most of my time on the small sofa by the window, near a floor lamp and air conditioner. Listening to the tapes my friends had given me when I left, I felt the happiness and security of a lost traveler who has found a familiar trail.

School came and dragged me out of my corner, drowning me in new terms and concepts. Work proved an effective cure for nostalgia: concentrating on immediate tasks prevented me from falling back into despair.

The crippling language barrier was rapidly thinning out. One day in my history class, in the middle of a discussion on the origins of writing, I caught myself listening and speaking English without first translating from Russian. The words were imprinted directly on my mind, invoking definite images. I had learned to think in English.

As time flowed by, depositing a layer of new impressions on my mind, I grew increasingly accustomed to my new life. Schoolmates started greeting me in the streets, flashing a quick smile as I passed by, and I smiled back. I was really getting used to my new life.

> *Time is a never-ending rain*
> *That hits at random roofs and faces.*
> *Whatever comes, don't grieve in vain:*
> *The rain will wash away all traces...*

These are the words of a song by one of my

In January of 1994, U.S. President Bill Clinton met with Russian President Boris Yeltsin. The Clintons became the first First Family to sleep at the Kremlin.

favorite Russian folk singers, Vadim Yegorov. Today, they hold a very special meaning for me.

Gradually, my hostility and negative response toward everything American faded away. So far, I have not become a baseball fan or started carrying a Walkman; but I no longer feel disgust at seeing my brother sit on a table or hearing him say an English word. And to the timeless question, "Where are you from?" I now answer, "From Boston." Through five years of struggle, I have earned this right.◆

Glossary

cold war Conflict characterized by the use of means short of overt military action.

communism Social organization in which goods are held in common.

coup Sudden violent overthrow of a government by a small group.

dysfunctional Not operating properly.

oppression Unjust or cruel exercise of power.

perestroika Former Soviet President Mikhail Gorbachev's proposed economic reforms.

private enterprise Business endeavor undertaken by an individual or group of individuals.

propaganda The spreading of ideas or information to support or damage a cause.

Refusenik A Soviet citizen who is refused permission to emigrate from Russia.

socialism A theory of social organization based on government control of production, distribution, and exchange of goods.

stagnation Dullness or inactivity.

tsar The ruler of Russia until 1917.

For Further Reading

Acton, Edward. *Rethinking the Russian Revolution.* New York: Routledge, Chapman, and Hall, 1990.

Adelman, Deborah. *The Children of Perestroika: Moscow Teenagers Talk about Their Lives and the Future.* Armonk, NY: M.E. Sharpe, Inc., 1991.

Beschloss, Michael R. *At the Highest Levels: The Inside Story of the End of the Cold War.* Boston: Little, Brown, 1993.

Caulkins, Janet. *The Picture Life of Mikhail Gorbachev.* New York: Franklin Watts, 1985.

Drachman, Edward R. *Challenging the Kremlin: The Soviet Jewish Movement for Freedom.* New York: Paragon House, 1991.

Smith, Hedrick. *The New Russians*, rev. ed. New York: Random House, 1991.

Yeltsin, Boris Nikolayevich. *The Struggle for Russia.* New York: Times Books, 1994.

Index

ACKNOWLEDGMENTS

I would like to thank Nina Baren and Alla Landa for their assistance with this book.

ABOUT THE AUTHOR

Tatyana Zamenova is a native of Moscow. She came to the United States to study at the University of Washington, where she is currently working on her Ph.D. in Russian literature. Ms. Zemenova lives in Seattle with her husband.

PHOTO CREDITS

cover photo and p.10 © Mimi Cotter/Int'l Stock Photos; p. 14, 16, 43, 47, 54 © Jeff Greenberg/Int'l Stock Photos; all other photos © AP/Wide World Photos.

LAYOUT AND DESIGN

Kim Sonsky